Month...

F...

The Monthly Marketi... you co-ordinate your ... different platforms, tying together your blogs, email marketing and social media to create a joined up marketing strategy for the coming year. It is undated so you can pick it up and put is down as needed without feeling like you've missed a month. At the back of the journal there is a list of monthly awareness days and daily hashtags to help you focus on things that are relevant to your business.

The Annual Marketing Planner includes a monthly email with tips and encouragement.

You can sign up to receive the emails using the QR code below.

Plan your blogs ahead to focus your marketing efforts and make your life easier when considering what to post to social media. Joining up your marketing strategy gives a focused overview that will tell your customers exactly what you do and how you can help them.

Include at least four social media posts over the month that point back to your blog, this will bring people across to your website, where you want them so they can see what else you can do for them.

Use snippets from the blog to generate interest in reading the whole thing.

Plan at least a monthly email newsletter to your contacts and include a link to your blog, give them some general information and any updates on your products and services. If you don't yet have an email list then look at ways to build one using opt in methods such as pop ups and lead magnets to get yourself an engaged and interested audience.

A lot of people find it hard to decide what to put on social media and then back away and say nothing. So it doesn't seem overwhelming try for at least 3 posts a week. It's better to plan a few weeks content at a time, sit down and put together a mixture of engaging posts mixed with a bit of selling, ask a few questions and be real, tell them about what you're getting up to today.

There are lots of different ways to schedule ahead to social media, if you're focused on Facebook and Instagram then try Facebook's Business Suite, which is free, built in and publishes to both sites at once.

Paying for platforms like Smarterqueue and MeetEdgar will provide evergreen content scheduling that means that you can prepare a few posts that repeat regularly, but intersperse them with plenty of new content.

Month:

Blog Planning

Think of a topic for your blog. Base it on your current focus, and tie it into your monthly email and social media plans for the month. This way your marketing is joined up and giving a cohesive story across all platforms.

Title:

Content Notes:

_____
_____
_____
_____
_____
_____
_____
_____

Email Marketing Planning

Plan time in your diary each month to send out an email to everyone on your list. If you don't have a list then think about building one. They are an invaluable resource for your marketing. Share your blog, your news and updates about products and services.

Title:

Content Notes:

_____
_____
_____
_____
_____
_____
_____
_____

Social Media Planning

Facebook followers at the start of the month

Instagram followers at the start of the month

Top 3 performing posts from the previous month:

1.
2.
3.

INSTAGRAM PLANNER

MONDAY	TUESDAY	WEDNESDAY	THURSDAY	FRIDAY	SATURDAY	SUNDAY

MONTHLY FOCUS

LINKEDIN PLANNER

NOTES:

Month:

_____

Blog Planning

Think of a topic for your blog. Base it on your current focus, and tie it into your monthly email and social media plans for the month. This way your marketing is joined up and giving a cohesive story across all platforms.

Title:

Content Notes:

_____
_____
_____
_____
_____
_____
_____
_____

Email Marketing Planning

Plan time in your diary each month to send out an email to everyone on your list. If you don't have a list then think about building one. They are an invaluable resource for your marketing. Share your blog, your news and updates about products and services.

Title:

Content Notes:

_____
_____
_____
_____
_____
_____
_____
_____

Social Media Planning

Facebook followers at the start of the month

Instagram followers at the start of the month

Top 3 performing posts from the previous month:

1.
2.
3.

NOTES:

Month:

_____

Blog Planning

Think of a topic for your blog. Base it on your current focus, and tie it into your monthly email and social media plans for the month. This way your marketing is joined up and giving a cohesive story across all platforms.

Title:

Content Notes:

_____
_____
_____
_____
_____
_____
_____
_____
_____
_____

Email Marketing Planning

Plan time in your diary each month to send out an email to everyone on your list. If you don't have a list then think about building one. They are an invaluable resource for your marketing. Share your blog, your news and updates about products and services.

Title:

Content Notes:

_____
_____
_____
_____
_____
_____
_____
_____
_____

Social Media Planning

Facebook followers at the start of the month

Instagram followers at the start of the month

Top 3 performing posts from the previous month:

1.
2.
3.

LINKEDIN PLANNER

MONDAY	TUESDAY	WEDNESDAY	THURSDAY	FRIDAY	SATURDAY	SUNDAY

MONTHLY FOCUS

NOTES:

Month:

___

Blog Planning

Think of a topic for your blog. Base it on your current focus, and tie it into your monthly email and social media plans for the month. This way your marketing is joined up and giving a cohesive story across all platforms.

Title:

Content Notes:

_____
_____
_____
_____
_____
_____
_____
_____

Email Marketing Planning

Plan time in your diary each month to send out an email to everyone on your list. If you don't have a list then think about building one. They are an invaluable resource for your marketing. Share your blog, your news and updates about products and services.

Title:

Content Notes:

_____

_____

_____

_____

_____

_____

_____

_____

Social Media Planning

Facebook followers at the start of the month

Instagram followers at the start of the month

Top 3 performing posts from the previous month:

1.
2.
3.

FACEBOOK PLANNER

MONDAY	TUESDAY	WEDNESDAY	THURSDAY	FRIDAY	SATURDAY	SUNDAY

MONTHLY FOCUS

INSTAGRAM PLANNER

NOTES:

Month:

___

Blog Planning

Think of a topic for your blog. Base it on your current focus, and tie it into your monthly email and social media plans for the month. This way your marketing is joined up and giving a cohesive story across all platforms.

Title:

Content Notes:

_____
_____
_____
_____
_____
_____
_____
_____

Email Marketing Planning

Plan time in your diary each month to send out an email to everyone on your list. If you don't have a list then think about building one. They are an invaluable resource for your marketing. Share your blog, your news and updates about products and services.

Title:

Content Notes:

_____
_____
_____
_____
_____
_____
_____
_____

Social Media Planning

Facebook followers at the start of the month

Instagram followers at the start of the month

Top 3 performing posts from the previous month:

1.
2.
3.

FACEBOOK PLANNER

MONDAY	TUESDAY	WEDNESDAY	THURSDAY	FRIDAY	SATURDAY	SUNDAY

MONTHLY FOCUS

INSTAGRAM PLANNER

MONDAY	TUESDAY	WEDNESDAY	THURSDAY	FRIDAY	SATURDAY	SUNDAY

MONTHLY FOCUS

LINKEDIN PLANNER

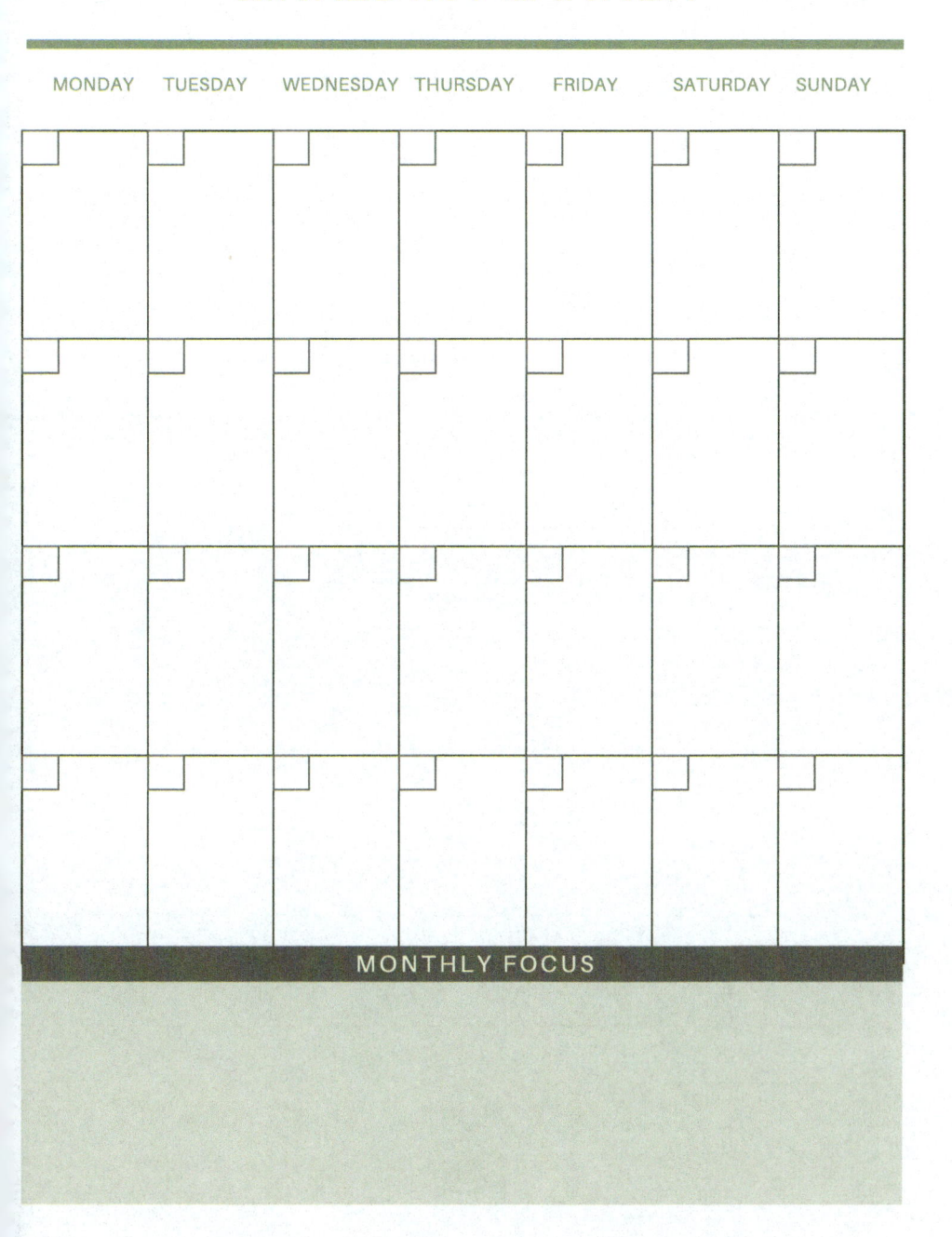

MONDAY	TUESDAY	WEDNESDAY	THURSDAY	FRIDAY	SATURDAY	SUNDAY

MONTHLY FOCUS

NOTES:

Month:

_____

Blog Planning

Think of a topic for your blog. Base it on your current focus, and tie it into your monthly email and social media plans for the month. This way your marketing is joined up and giving a cohesive story across all platforms.

Title:

Content Notes:

_____
_____
_____
_____
_____
_____
_____
_____

Email Marketing Planning

Plan time in your diary each month to send out an email to everyone on your list. If you don't have a list then think about building one. They are an invaluable resource for your marketing. Share your blog, your news and updates about products and services.

Title:

Content Notes:

_____

_____

_____

_____

_____

_____

_____

_____

Social Media Planning

Facebook followers at the start of the month

Instagram followers at the start of the month

Top 3 performing posts from the previous month:

1.
2.
3.

FACEBOOK PLANNER

MONDAY	TUESDAY	WEDNESDAY	THURSDAY	FRIDAY	SATURDAY	SUNDAY

MONTHLY FOCUS

INSTAGRAM PLANNER

MONDAY	TUESDAY	WEDNESDAY	THURSDAY	FRIDAY	SATURDAY	SUNDAY

MONTHLY FOCUS

LINKEDIN PLANNER

MONDAY	TUESDAY	WEDNESDAY	THURSDAY	FRIDAY	SATURDAY	SUNDAY

MONTHLY FOCUS

NOTES:

Month:

_____

Blog Planning

Think of a topic for your blog. Base it on your current focus, and tie it into your monthly email and social media plans for the month. This way your marketing is joined up and giving a cohesive story across all platforms.

Title:

Content Notes:

_____
_____
_____
_____
_____
_____
_____
_____

Email Marketing Planning

Plan time in your diary each month to send out an email to everyone on your list. If you don't have a list then think about building one. They are an invaluable resource for your marketing. Share your blog, your news and updates about products and services.

Title:

Content Notes:

_____

_____

_____

_____

_____

_____

_____

_____

Social Media Planning

Facebook followers at the start of the month

Instagram followers at the start of the month

Top 3 performing posts from the previous month:

1.
2.
3.

FACEBOOK PLANNER

MONDAY	TUESDAY	WEDNESDAY	THURSDAY	FRIDAY	SATURDAY	SUNDAY

MONTHLY FOCUS

INSTAGRAM PLANNER

MONDAY	TUESDAY	WEDNESDAY	THURSDAY	FRIDAY	SATURDAY	SUNDAY

MONTHLY FOCUS

LINKEDIN PLANNER

MONDAY	TUESDAY	WEDNESDAY	THURSDAY	FRIDAY	SATURDAY	SUNDAY

MONTHLY FOCUS

NOTES:

Month:

_____

Blog Planning

Think of a topic for your blog. Base it on your current focus, and tie it into your monthly email and social media plans for the month. This way your marketing is joined up and giving a cohesive story across all platforms.

Title:

Content Notes:

_____
_____
_____
_____
_____
_____
_____
_____
_____

Email Marketing Planning

Plan time in your diary each month to send out an email to everyone on your list. If you don't have a list then think about building one. They are an invaluable resource for your marketing. Share your blog, your news and updates about products and services.

Title:

Content Notes:

_____
_____
_____
_____
_____
_____
_____
_____

Social Media Planning

Facebook followers at the start of the month

Instagram followers at the start of the month

Top 3 performing posts from the previous month:

1.
2.
3.

FACEBOOK PLANNER

MONDAY	TUESDAY	WEDNESDAY	THURSDAY	FRIDAY	SATURDAY	SUNDAY

MONTHLY FOCUS

INSTAGRAM PLANNER

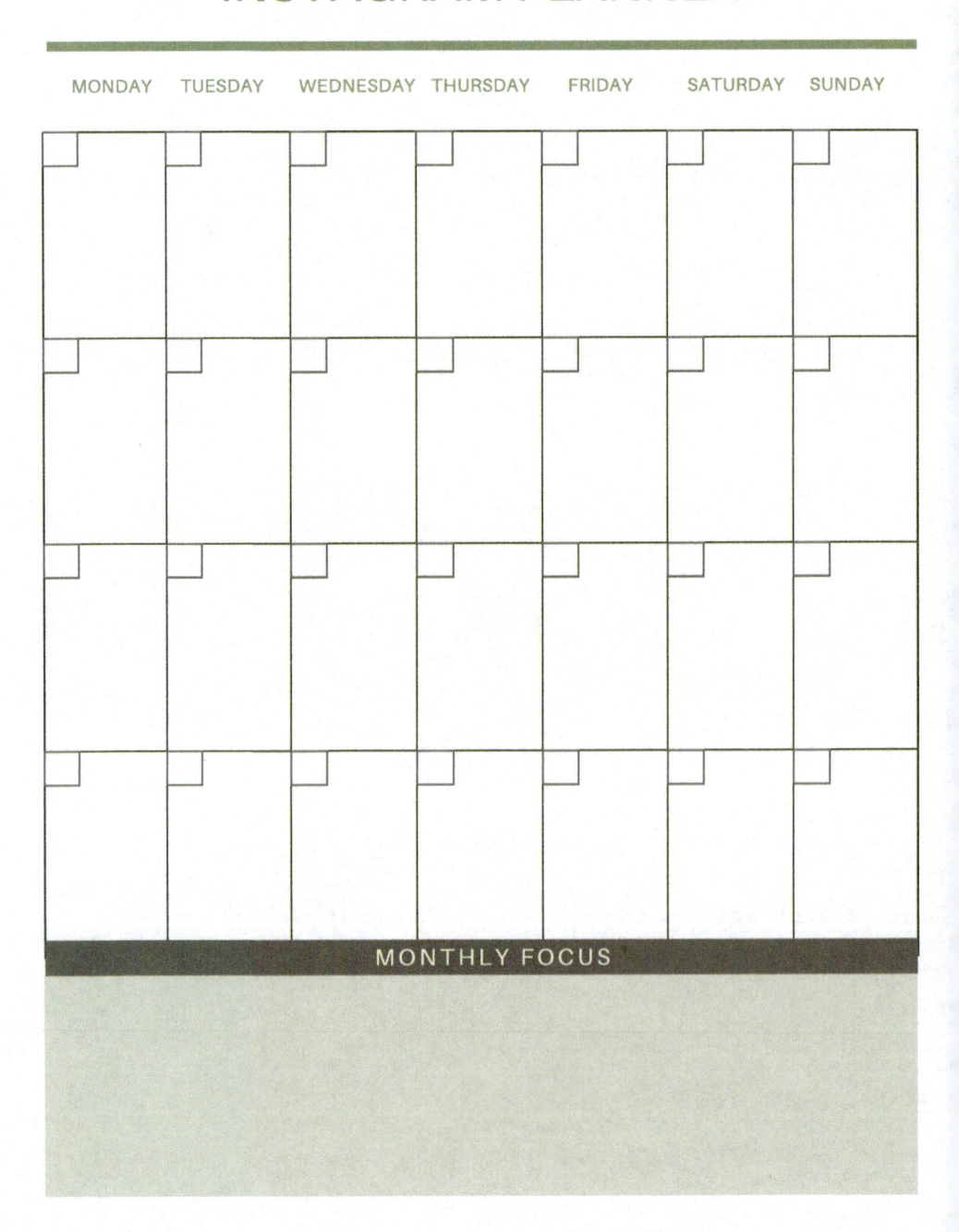

MONDAY	TUESDAY	WEDNESDAY	THURSDAY	FRIDAY	SATURDAY	SUNDAY

MONTHLY FOCUS

LINKEDIN PLANNER

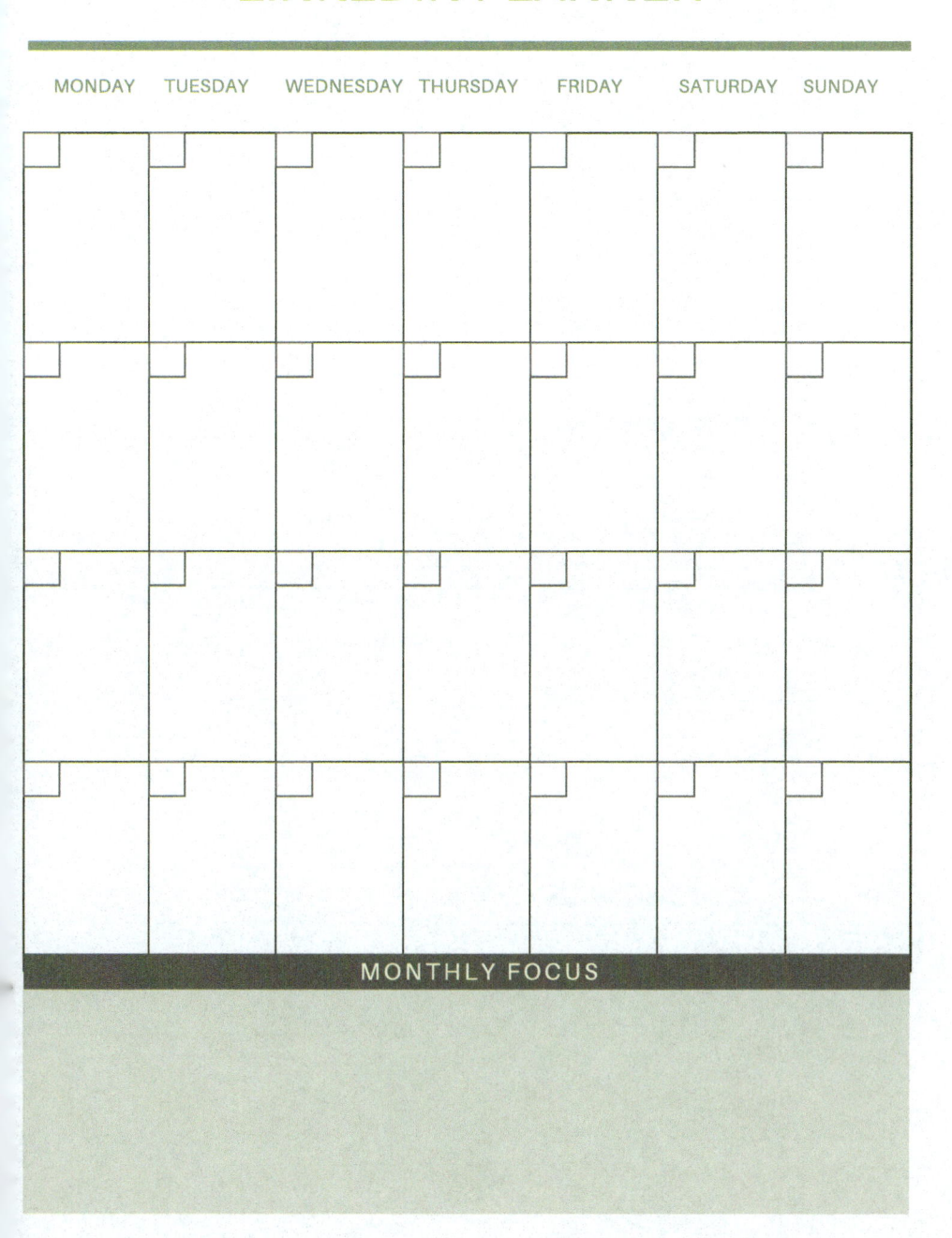

MONDAY	TUESDAY	WEDNESDAY	THURSDAY	FRIDAY	SATURDAY	SUNDAY

MONTHLY FOCUS

NOTES:

Month:

_____

Blog Planning

Think of a topic for your blog. Base it on your current focus, and tie it into your monthly email and social media plans for the month. This way your marketing is joined up and giving a cohesive story across all platforms.

Title:

Content Notes:

_____
_____
_____
_____
_____
_____
_____
_____

Email Marketing Planning

Plan time in your diary each month to send out an email to everyone on your list. If you don't have a list then think about building one. They are an invaluable resource for your marketing. Share your blog, your news and updates about products and services.

Title:

Content Notes:

_____
_____
_____
_____
_____
_____
_____
_____

Social Media Planning

Facebook followers at the start of the month

Instagram followers at the start of the month

Top 3 performing posts from the previous month:

1.
2.
3.

FACEBOOK PLANNER

MONDAY	TUESDAY	WEDNESDAY	THURSDAY	FRIDAY	SATURDAY	SUNDAY

MONTHLY FOCUS

INSTAGRAM PLANNER

MONDAY	TUESDAY	WEDNESDAY	THURSDAY	FRIDAY	SATURDAY	SUNDAY

MONTHLY FOCUS

LINKEDIN PLANNER

MONDAY	TUESDAY	WEDNESDAY	THURSDAY	FRIDAY	SATURDAY	SUNDAY

MONTHLY FOCUS

NOTES:

Month:

_____

Blog Planning

Think of a topic for your blog. Base it on your current focus, and tie it into your monthly email and social media plans for the month. This way your marketing is joined up and giving a cohesive story across all platforms.

Title:

Content Notes:

_____
_____
_____
_____
_____
_____
_____
_____

Email Marketing Planning

Plan time in your diary each month to send out an email to everyone on your list. If you don't have a list then think about building one. They are an invaluable resource for your marketing. Share your blog, your news and updates about products and services.

Title:

Content Notes:

_____
_____
_____
_____
_____
_____
_____
_____

Social Media Planning

Facebook followers at the start of the month

Instagram followers at the start of the month

Top 3 performing posts from the previous month:

1.
2.
3.

FACEBOOK PLANNER

MONDAY	TUESDAY	WEDNESDAY	THURSDAY	FRIDAY	SATURDAY	SUNDAY

MONTHLY FOCUS

INSTAGRAM PLANNER

MONDAY	TUESDAY	WEDNESDAY	THURSDAY	FRIDAY	SATURDAY	SUNDAY

MONTHLY FOCUS

LINKEDIN PLANNER

MONDAY	TUESDAY	WEDNESDAY	THURSDAY	FRIDAY	SATURDAY	SUNDAY

MONTHLY FOCUS

NOTES:

Month:

Blog Planning

Think of a topic for your blog. Base it on your current focus, and tie it into your monthly email and social media plans for the month. This way your marketing is joined up and giving a cohesive story across all platforms.

Title:

Content Notes:

_____
_____
_____
_____
_____
_____
_____
_____

Email Marketing Planning

Plan time in your diary each month to send out an email to everyone on your list. If you don't have a list then think about building one. They are an invaluable resource for your marketing. Share your blog, your news and updates about products and services.

Title:

Content Notes:

_____
_____
_____
_____
_____
_____
_____
_____

Social Media Planning

Facebook followers at the start of the month

Instagram followers at the start of the month

Top 3 performing posts from the previous month:

1.
2.
3.

FACEBOOK PLANNER

MONDAY	TUESDAY	WEDNESDAY	THURSDAY	FRIDAY	SATURDAY	SUNDAY

MONTHLY FOCUS

INSTAGRAM PLANNER

MONDAY	TUESDAY	WEDNESDAY	THURSDAY	FRIDAY	SATURDAY	SUNDAY

MONTHLY FOCUS

LINKEDIN PLANNER

MONDAY	TUESDAY	WEDNESDAY	THURSDAY	FRIDAY	SATURDAY	SUNDAY

MONTHLY FOCUS

NOTES:

Month:

_____

Blog Planning

Think of a topic for your blog. Base it on your current focus, and tie it into your monthly email and social media plans for the month. This way your marketing is joined up and giving a cohesive story across all platforms.

Title:

Content Notes:

_____
_____
_____
_____
_____
_____
_____
_____

Email Marketing Planning

Plan time in your diary each month to send out an email to everyone on your list. If you don't have a list then think about building one. They are an invaluable resource for your marketing. Share your blog, your news and updates about products and services.

Title:

Content Notes:

_____
_____
_____
_____
_____
_____
_____
_____

Social Media Planning

Facebook followers at the start of the month

Instagram followers at the start of the month

Top 3 performing posts from the previous month:

1.
2.
3.

FACEBOOK PLANNER

MONDAY	TUESDAY	WEDNESDAY	THURSDAY	FRIDAY	SATURDAY	SUNDAY

MONTHLY FOCUS

INSTAGRAM PLANNER

MONDAY	TUESDAY	WEDNESDAY	THURSDAY	FRIDAY	SATURDAY	SUNDAY

MONTHLY FOCUS

LINKEDIN PLANNER

MONDAY	TUESDAY	WEDNESDAY	THURSDAY	FRIDAY	SATURDAY	SUNDAY

MONTHLY FOCUS

NOTES:

Daily Hashtags and Monthly Awareness Days

Using the Daily Hashtags will help you plan posts that can be easily searched by others looking for those hashtags. Some are more popular than others and will have a lot more posts under that hashtag and a bigger following of people. Hashtags such as #Motivational Monday and #FollowFriday will have a large following and help you to be easily found by a larger audience.

There are hundreds of monthly awareness days to choose from, the lists following are based on 2022, if you are using this planner beyond that date than double check the lists, just in case the awareness day has moved. Sometimes the event is tied to the date and other times to the actual day. They will also usually have a hashtag associated so look that up and add it to your post. Choose awareness days taht in some way link back to your business or your interests, don't just use every single one for the sake of them. They should have some relevancy to you in some way.

For more ideas visit hashtagpicker.com or for National Awareness Days visit www.awarenessdays.com

Daily Hashtags

#MondayMotivation
#MondayBlues
#MusicMonday
#MagicMonday
#MondayBlog
#MeatFreeMonday

#WednesdayWisdom
#HumpDay
#WednesdayWorkout
#WayBackWednesday
#WineWednesday
#WoofWednesday

#FridayFeeling
#FeelGoodFriday
#FollowFriday or #FF
#FridayFun
#TGIF
#HappyFriday

#LazySunday
#SelflessSunday
#SelfieSunday
#SundayFun
#ScienceSunday
#SundayBlogShare

#TipTuesday
#TuesdayThoughts
#CharityTuesday
#TransformationTuesday
#TravelTuesday
#TestimonialTuesday

#ThrowbackThursday
#ThankfulThursday
#ThursdayThoughts
#Thursdate
#ArtThursday
#CoffeeThursday

#ShoutoutSaturday
#SocialSaturday
#SaturdaySelfie
#SaturdayShenanigans
#StreetSaturday

Awareness Days
January

1 JANUARY
NEW YEAR'S DAY
DRY JANUARY
VEGANUARY
WALK YOUR DOG MONTH
2 JANUARY
BUFFET DAY
SCIENCE FICTION DAY
3 JANUARY
FESTIVAL OF SLEEP DAY
4 JANUARY
WORLD BRAILLE DAY
7 JANUARY
OLD ROCK DAY
9 JANUARY
WORD NERD DAY
10 JANUARY
CLEAN YOUR DESK DAY
11 JANUARY
PAGET'S AWARENESS DAY
16 JANUARY
WORLD RELIGION DAY
17 JANUARY
MARTIN LUTHER KING DAY
BLUE MONDAY
CERVICAL CANCER PREVENTION WEEK
18 JANUARY
BIG ENERGY SAVING WEEK
WINNIE THE POOH DAY
THESAURUS DAY

19 JANUARY
NATIONAL POPCORN DAY
20 JANUARY
GET TO KNOW YOUR CUSTOMERS DAY
21 JANUARY
NATIONAL HUG DAY
SQUIRREL APPRECIATION DAY
23 JANUARY
NATIONAL PIE DAY
HAND WRITING DAY
24 JANUARY
COMPLIMENT DAY
25 JANUARY
BURNS NIGHT
26 JANUARY
AUSTRALIA DAY
27 JANUARY
HOLOCAUST MEMORIAL DAY
CHOCOLATE CAKE DAY
28 JANUARY
DATA PRIVACY DAY
29 JANUARY
PUZZLE DAY
30 JANUARY
CROISSANT DAY
NATIONAL STORYTELLING WEEK

Awareness Days
February

1 FEBRUARY
LGBT+ HISTORY MONTH
CHINESE NEW YEAR - YEAR OF THE TIGER
2 FEBRUARY
WORLD WETLANDS DAY
PLAY YOUR UKULELE DAY
3 FEBRUARY
TIME TO TALK DAY
4 FEBRUARY
WORLD CANCER DAY
WORK NAKED DAY
5 FEBRUARY
WORLD NUTELLA DAY
EAT ICE CREAM FOR BREAKFAST DAY
7 FEBRUARY
SEND A CARD TO A FRIEND DAY
CHILDREN'S MENTAL HEATH WEEK
TINNITUS AWARENESS WEEK
NATIONAL SICKIE DAY
8 FEBRUARY
SAFER INTERNET DAY
9 FEBRUARY
NATIONAL PIZZA DAY
TOOTHACHE DAY
10 FEBRUARY
UMBRELLA DAY
11 FEBRUARY
DON'T CRY OVER SPILLED MILK DAY
MAKE A FRIEND DAY

14 FEBRUARY
VALENTINE'S DAY
INTERNATIONAL BOOK GIVING DAY
LIBRARY LOVERS DAY
INTERNATIONAL EPILEPSY DAY
15 FEBRUARY
GUMDROP DAY
17 FEBRUARY
RANDOM ACTS OF KINDNESS DAY
18 FEBRUARY
CARE DAY
19 FEBRUARY
REAL BREAD WEEK
20 FEBRUARY
NATIONAL LOVE YOUR PET DAY
21 FEBRUARY
FAIRTRADE FORTNIGHT
22 FEBRUARY
WORLD THINKING DAY
26 FEBRUARY
TELL A FAIRY TALE DAY
28 FEBRUARY
PUBLIC SLEEPING DAY
RARE DISEASE DAY

Awareness Days
March

1 MARCH
SHROVE TUESDAY
TIME FOR A CUPPA - DEMENTIA UK
ST DAVID'S DAY
OVARIAN CANCER AWARENESS MONTH
SELF INJURY/HARM AWARENESS DAY

2 MARCH
NATIONAL OLD STUFF DAY

4 MARCH
MARCH FORTH AND DO SOMETHING DAY
UNIVERSITY MENTAL HEALTH DAY
NATIONAL EMPLOYEE APPRECIATION DAY

5 MARCH
BRITISH SCIENCE WEEK

7 MARCH
BRITISH PIE WEEK
NATIONAL CAREERS WEEK

8 MARCH
NATIONAL BUTCHERS WEEK
INTERNATIONAL WOMEN'S DAY
PROOFREADING DAY

10 MARCH
NATIONAL NO SMOKING DAY

14 MARCH
NUTRITION AND HYDRATION WEEK

15 MARCH
WORLD CONSUMER RIGHTS DAY

17 MARCH
ST PATRICKS DAY

18 MARCH
WORLD SLEEP DAY
COMIC RELIEF RED NOSE DAY

20 MARCH
SPRING EQUINOX (FIRST DAY OF SPRING)
WORLD ORAL HEALTH DAY
INTERNATIONAL DAY OF HAPPINESS
NATIONAL COMPLEMENTARY THERAPY WEEK

21 MARCH
INTERNATIONAL DAY OF FORESTS
WORLD POETRY DAY

23 MARCH
WORLD METEOROLOGICAL DAY
NATIONAL WORKOUTS AND WELLBEING WEEK

26 MARCH
YOUNG EPILEPSY PURPLE DAY

27 MARCH
WORLD THEATRE DAY
MOTHERING SUNDAY

30 MARCH
WORLD BIPOLAR DAY
TAKE A WALK IN THE PARK DAY

31 MARCH
INTERNATIONAL TRANS DAY OF VISIBILITY

Awareness Days
April

1 APRIL
APRIL FOOLS DAY
IBS AWARENESS MONTH
JAZZ APPRECIATION MONTH
PARKINSON'S AWARENESS MONTH
INTERNATIONAL CESAREAN AWARENESS MONTH
NATIONAL PET MONTH
WALK TO WORK DAY

2 APRIL
WORLD AUTISM AWARENESS DAY
INTERNATIONAL CHILDREN'S BOOK DAY
INTERNATIONAL PILLOW FIGHT DAY

7 APRIL
WORLD HEALTH DAY

10 APRIL
NATIONAL SIBLINGS DAY
WORLD HOMEOPATHY AWARENESS WEEK

11 APRIL
WORLD PARKINSON'S DAY
NATIONAL PET DAY

13 APRIL
INTERNATIONAL FND AWARENESS DAY
SCRABBLE DAY

15 APRIL
INTERNATIONAL MICROVOLUNTEERING DAY
GOOD FRIDAY

16 APRIL
WORLD VOICE DAY

17 APRIL
WORLD HAEMOPHILIA DAY
EASTER SUNDAY

18 APRIL
EASTER MONDAY

19 APRIL
NATIONAL WEAR YOUR PYJAMAS TO WORK DAY

20 APRIL
LOOK ALIKE DAY

22 APRIL
INTERNATIONAL MOTHER EARTH DAY

23 APRIL
ST GEORGE'S DAY
ENGLISH LANGUAGE DAY
WORLD BOOK NIGHT
TAKE A CHANCE DAY

24 APRIL
NATIONAL SKIPPING DAY

25 APRIL
WORLD PENGUIN DAY

26 APRIL
WORLD IP DAY

28 APRIL
WORLD DAY FOR SAFETY AND HEALTH AT WORK

29 APRIL
INTERNATIONAL DANCE DAY

30 APRIL
INTERNATIONAL JAZZ DAY
HONESTY DAY

Awareness Days
May

1 MAY
MAY MEASUREMENT MONTH
INTERNATIONAL DAWN CHORUS DAY
2 MAY
MAY DAY
3 MAY
WORLD ASTHMA DAY
4 MAY
STAR WARS DAY
5 MAY
INTERNATIONAL DAY OF THE MIDWIFE
8 MAY
WORLD OVARIAN CANCER DAY
NATIONAL AMYLOIDOSIS DAY
9 MAY
LOST SOCK MEMORIAL DAY
EUROPE DAY
11 MAY
EAT WHAT YOU WANT DAY
12 MAY
ME AWARENESS DAY
14 MAY
DANCE LIKE A CHICKEN DAY
WORLD FAIRTRADE DAY
15 MAY
INTERNATIONAL DAY OF FAMILIES
17 MAY
WORLD HYPERTENSION DAY
18 MAY
INTERNATIONAL MUSEUMS DAY

21 MAY
WORLD MEDITATION DAY
WORLD DAY FOR CULTURAL DIVERSITY
TALK LIKE YODA DAY
23 MAY
WORLD TURTLE DAY
25 MAY
INTERNATIONAL MISSING CHILDREN'S DAY
27 MAY
SUN SCREEN DAY
28 MAY
GREAT BRITISH SPRING CLEAN
29 MAY
NATIONAL BISCUIT DAY
30 MAY
WORLD MS DAY

Awareness Days
June

1 JUNE
SAY SOMETHING NICE DAY
INTERNATIONAL CHILDREN'S DAY
GLOBAL DAY OF PARENTS
WORLD MILK DAY
2 JUNE
SPRING BANK HOLIDAY
LEAVE THE OFFICE EARLY DAY
3 JUNE
NATIONAL DONUT DAY
4 JUNE
HUG YOUR CAT DAY
NATIONAL CHEESE DAY
5 JUNE
WORLD ENVIRONMENT DAY
CANCER SURVIVORS DAY
7 JUNE
TOURETTES AWARENESS DAY
AROMATHERAPY AWARENESS WEEK
8 JUNE
NATIONAL BEST FRIENDS DAY
WORLD OCEANS DAY
10 JUNE
MEN'S HEALTH WEEK
11 JUNE
CORN ON THE COB DAY
12 JUNE
RED ROSE DAY
13 JUNE
SEWING MACHINE DAY
14 JUNE
WORLD BLOOD DONOR DAY
15 JUNE
NATIONAL BUG BUSTING DAY
17 JUNE
WORLD DAY TO COMBAT DESERTIFICATION AND DROUGHT
18 JUNE
INTERNATIONAL PICNIC DAY
NATIONAL PICNIC WEEK
SUSTAINABLE GASTRONOMY DAY
19 JUNE
WORLD JUGGLING DAY
FATHERS DAY
21 JUNE
FIRST DAY OF SUMMER - SUMMER SOLSTICE
INTERNATIONAL SURFING DAY
WORLD HUMANIST DAY
GLOBAL MND AWARENESS DAY
WORLD MUSIC DAY
NATIONAL SELFIE DAY
23 JUNE
TYPEWRITER DAY
26 JUNE
CHOCOLATE PUDDING DAY
27 JUNE
INTERNATIONAL SUNGLASSES DAY
30 JUNE
SOCIAL MEDIA DAY
NATIONAL METEOR WATCH DAY

Awareness Days
July

1 JULY
NATIONAL PICNIC MONTH
PLASTIC FREE JULY
INTERNATIONAL REGGAE DAY
INTERNATIONAL JOKE DAY
3 JULY
INTERNATIONAL PLASTIC BAG FREE DAY
COMPLIMENT YOUR MIRROR DAY
4 JULY
AMERICAN INDEPENDENCE DAY
5 JULY
WORKAHOLICS DAY
6 JULY
INTERNATIONAL KISSING DAY
7 JULY
WORLD CHOCOLATE DAY
TELL THE TRUTH DAY
10 JULY
DON'T STEP ON A BEE DAY
TEDDY BEARS' PICNIC DAY
12 JULY
NATIONAL SIMPLICITY DAY
13 JULY
EMBRACE YOUR GEEKNESS DAY
15 JULY
WORLD YOUTH SKILLS DAY
GIVE SOMETHING AWAY DAY
17 JULY
WORLD EMOJI DAY

19 JULY
STICK OUT YOUR TONGUE DAY
21 JULY
JUNK FOOD DAY
24 JULY
NATIONAL TEQUILA DAY
NATIONAL FISHING MONTH
28 JULY
MILK CHOCOLATE DAY
29 JULY
INTERNATIONAL TIGER DAY
30 JULY
INTERNATIONAL FRIENDSHIP DAY
NATIONAL CHEESECAKE DAY

Awareness Days
August

1 AUGUST
WORLD BREASTFEEDING WEEK
YORKSHIRE DAY
3 AUGUST
WATERMELON DAY
8 AUGUST
INTERNATIONAL CAT DAY
9 AUGUST
NATIONAL BOOK LOVERS DAY
10 AUGUST
NATIONAL LAZY DAY
12 AUGUST
INTERNATIONAL YOUTH DAY
MIDDLE CHILD DAY
13 AUGUST
NATIONAL PROSECCO DAY
LEFT HANDERS AWARENESS DAY
15 AUGUST
NATIONAL RELAXATION DAY
16 AUGUST
TELL A JOKE DAY
19 AUGUST
WORLD PHOTO DAY

25 AUGUST
KISS AND MAKE UP DAY
26 AUGUST
DOG APPRECIATION DAY
28 AUGUST
BOW TIE DAY
29 AUGUST
SUMMER BANK HOLIDAY
31 AUGUST
EAT OUTSIDE DAY

Awareness Days
September

1 SEPTEMBER
SOURDOUGH SEPTEMBER
WORLD ALZHEIMER MONTH
ORGANIC SEPTEMBER
FESTIVAL OF LEARNING HAVE A GO MONTH
WALKING TOGETHER - BLOOD CANCER
CHILDHOOD CANCER AWARENESS MONTH
WORLD FUNFAIR MONTH

3 SEPTEMBER
EVERYWOMAN DAY
NATIONAL DOODLE DAY

4 SEPTEMBER
INTERNATIONAL BACON DAY

5 SEPTEMBER
INTERNATIONAL DAY OF CHARITY
MIGRAINE AWARENESS WEEK

6 SEPTEMBER
READ A BOOK DAY
NATIONAL PAYROLL WEEK
KNOW YOUR NUMBERS WEEK (BLOOD PRESSURE UK)

7 SEPTEMBER
YOUR MENTAL HEALTH DAY

8 SEPTEMBER
INTERNATIONAL LITERACY DAY

10 SEPTEMBER
WORLD SUICIDE PREVENTION DAY
HERITAGE OPEN DAYS

13 SEPTEMBER
ROALD DAHL DAY
JEANS FOR GENES DAY
WORLD SEPSIS DAY
NATIONAL ECZEMA WEEK
RHEUMATOID ARTHRITIS (RA) AWARENESS WEEK
SEXUAL HEALTH WEEK

15 SEPTEMBER
PENSION AWARENESS DAY
INTERNATIONAL DOT DAY
WORLD LYMPHOMA AWARENESS DAY

16 SEPTEMBER
NATIONAL TEACHING ASSISTANTS DAY

17 SEPTEMBER
THE GREAT BRITISH BEACH CLEAN WEEK

19 SEPTEMBER
INTERNATIONAL TALK LIKE A PIRATE DAY

20 SEPTEMBER
NATIONAL EYE HEALTH WEEK
ORGAN DONATION WEEK
INTERNATIONAL WEEK OF HAPPINESS AT WORK
WORLD REFLEXOLOGY WEEK
RECYCLE WEEK

21 SEPTEMBER
INTERNATIONAL DAY OF PEACE
WORLD ALZHEIMER'S DAY

22 SEPTEMBER
WORLD CAR FREE DAY

24 SEPTEMBER
PUNCTUATION DAY
MACMILLAN WORLD'S BIGGEST COFFEE MORNING

26 SEPTEMBER
EUROPEAN DAY OF LANGUAGES

27 SEPTEMBER
WORLD TOURISM DAY
BIKE TO SCHOOL WEEK
INTERNATIONAL BABYWEARING WEEK

29 SEPTEMBER
WORLD HEART DAY
THANK YOU #HIDDENHEROES DAY

30 SEPTEMBER
NATIONAL SPORTING HERITAGE DAY

Awareness Days
October

1 OCTOBER
INTERNATIONAL COFFEE DAY
WORLD SMILE DAY
NATIONAL POETRY DAY
ADHD AWARENESS MONTH
BREAST CANCER AWARENESS MONTH
GO SOBER FOR OCTOBER
NATIONAL CHOLESTEROL MONTH
THE BIG DRAW
UNBLOCKTOBER
BLACK HISTORY MONTH
WORLD VEGETARIAN DAY
INTERNATIONAL WALK TO SCHOOL MONTH
INTERNATIONAL SCHOOL LIBRARY MONTH

2 OCTOBER
NATIONAL BRUNCH WEEKEND

4 OCTOBER
WORLD DYSLEXIA AWARENESS DAY
BYTE NIGHT
WORLD ANIMAL DAY
WORLD SPACE WEEK
NO DISPOSABLE CUP DAY
NATIONAL BABY SWIMMING WEEK

5 OCTOBER
INTERNATIONAL ASTRONOMY DAY
WORLD TEACHERS DAY

6 OCTOBER
DYSPRAXIA AWARENESS WEEK
NATIONAL BADGER DAY

7 OCTOBER
HUMPHREY'S PYJAMA WEEK
NATIONAL ARTHRITIS WEEK
NATIONAL CURRY WEEK

9 OCTOBER
BABY LOSS AWARENESS WEEK

10 OCTOBER
WORLD MENTAL HEALTH DAY

11 OCTOBER
INTERNATIONAL DAY OF THE GIRL CHILD
NATIONAL BRAILLE WEEK
NATIONAL COMING OUT DAY
WORLD PERIMENOPAUSE DAY

12 OCTOBER
INTERNATIONAL ANIMAL RIGHTS DAY (IARD)
NATIONAL WORK LIFE WEEK

13 OCTOBER
NATIONAL NO BRA DAY
WORLD SIGHT DAY

14 OCTOBER
CHOCOLATE WEEK
NATIONAL ADOPTION WEEK
NATIONAL BAKING WEEK

15 OCTOBER
WORLD VALUES DAY

16 OCTOBER
DICTIONARY DAY
FAMILY LEARNING FESTIVAL

18 OCTOBER
ANTI-SLAVERY DAY
WORLD MENOPAUSE DAY

28 OCTOBER
INTERNATIONAL ANIMATION DAY

29 OCTOBER
WORLD ONLINE NETWORKING DAY

31 OCTOBER
HALLOWE'EN
MUSEUMS AT NIGHT

Awareness Days
November

1 NOVEMBER
NATIONAL NOVEL WRITING MONTH
NATIONAL AUTHORS DAY
WORLD VEGAN DAY
MOVEMBER
INTERNATIONAL STRESS AWARENESS WEEK
NATIONAL CAREER DEVELOPMENT MONTH

3 NOVEMBER
NATIONAL SANDWICH DAY

4 NOVEMBER
NATIONAL PATHOLOGY WEEK
NATIONAL SPA WEEK

5 NOVEMBER
BONFIRE NIGHT

6 NOVEMBER
WORLD LET'S STOP SHOUTING DAY

9 NOVEMBER
WORLD FREEDOM DAY
SOCIAL MEDIA KINDNESS DAY

11 NOVEMBER
ARMISTICE DAY
ALCOHOL AWARENESS WEEK
ANTI-BULLYING WEEK

13 NOVEMBER
WORLD KINDNESS DAY

14 NOVEMBER
WORLD DIABETES DAY

16 NOVEMBER
NATIONAL ENTREPRENEURS DAY
WORLD NURSERY RHYME WEEK

20 NOVEMBER
UNIVERSAL CHILDREN'S DAY

24 NOVEMBER
CELEBRATE YOUR UNIQUE TALENT DAY

26 NOVEMBER
CAKE DAY
BLACK FRIDAY

27 NOVEMBER
SMALL BUSINESS SATURDAY

29 NOVEMBER
CYBER MONDAY

30 NOVEMBER
ST ANDREW'S DAY

Awareness Days
December

1 DECEMBER
DECEMBEARD
TREE DRESSING DAY
2 DECEMBER
NATIONAL GRIEF AWARENESS WEEK
3 DECEMBER
MAKE A GIFT DAY
4 DECEMBER
NATIONAL COOKIE DAY
WILDLIFE CONSERVATION DAY
5 DECEMBER
INTERNATIONAL VOLUNTEER DAY
7 DECEMBER
NATIONAL LETTER WRITING DAY
9 DECEMBER
CHRISTMAS CARD DAY
10 DECEMBER
HUMAN RIGHTS DAY
CHRISTMAS JUMPER DAY
12 DECEMBER
GINGERBREAD DECORATING DAY
NATIONAL WORKPLACE DAY OF REMEMBRANCE
15 DECEMBER
INTERNATIONAL TEA DAY
16 DECEMBER
CHOCOLATE COVERED ANYTHING DAY

17 DECEMBER
UNDERDOG DAY
INTERNATIONAL MIGRANTS DAY
21 DECEMBER
NATIONAL ROBIN DAY
24 DECEMBER
CHRISTMAS EVE
EGGNOG DAY
25 DECEMBER
CHRISTMAS DAY
26 DECEMBER
BOXING DAY
THANK YOU NOTE DAY
27 DECEMBER
NATIONAL FRUITCAKE DAY
28 DECEMBER
CARD PLAYING DAY
31 DECEMBER
NEW YEARS EVE

DRAGON
VIRTUAL ASSISTANTS LTD

www.dragonvirtualassistants.co.uk

Printed in Great Britain
by Amazon